Reverse Discrimination

The Minority Encounters of a Short White Boy

Fiction
The Author Murders: A Palm Springs Biblio-Mystery
The Witch of Tahquitz

Non-Fiction
Lawrence Welk's First Television Champagne Lady:
Roberta Linn
Not Now Lord, I've Got Too Much to Do
Reverse Discrimination:
The Minority Encounters of a Short White Boy

Edited by Eric G. Meeks
Facts & Legends of the Village of Palm Springs
Explorations and Surveys: Southwest Route for a Railroad

Amazon Short Stories
Mirth the Dragon versus the Book Dealer Knight
Apollo Thorn: A Sci-Fi Corporate Wars Story
The Vampire Diaries
Lucille Ball in Palm Springs or PS I Love Lucy

Reverse Discrimination

The Minority Encounters of a Short White Boy

Eric G. Meeks

Preface

It may not be a universal truth that Blacks, Mexicans, Orientals, Gays and Women have come to dominate the world, but in the sphere of influence empowering my world, it's become substantial. Although this has not always been so, the changes I've seen in race relations, within this country, is at times staggering.

I am told, as little as a generation and a half ago, the world was a much different place. During my parents' lifetime, which grew up in the Deep South of Arkansas and Louisiana, Blacks were not allowed to walk on the sidewalk. Fully grown black men and women would step off the pavement into the mud should even a white child be walking in their vicinity at the time. Drinking fountains and Movie theatre entrances were clearly marked for Whites only, or Blacks.

There is even a story in my family, of my Uncle Jesse, upon hearing a black man refer to him as Jesse, as opposed to sir or Mr. Meeks, that Uncle Jesse beat the black man so bad, he hid under a truck to prevent any further assault.

In my region of the United States, Southern California, there was a time when Mexicans were relegated to being farm workers and maids. Orientals were such a small minority their sections of the cities were novelties to be visited like an amusement park. Women were still looked down upon or insignificant in the workforce. It was not uncommon for a woman to have to sleep with her boss to get hired, advancement or a pay raise. As a matter of course, it was generally considered a bad sign for a family if the mom had to work.

As a child, the words Nigger, Spick, Wetback, and Chink were not uncommon for me to hear. Not so much from my parents, who I don't recall ever saying these words idly, but more so from my Grandmother, and her brothers (Uncle Jesse and Uncle Jimmie) and sisters (Aunt Susie and Aunt Dot). They were from two generations earlier than I and from a completely different world than even my parents.

My parents taught me these were words of hate and that they should not be spoken. While I have said these words a few times, I realize their meanings; the hatred, fear and suffering surrounding their usage and the reasons these words need to go away. But these words, their history, and the background they grew out of were from a world whose influence was waning by the time I came of age. Still, they are not extinct.

The hateful factors behind these words began to change during my lifetime. By the time I was an adult, occurrences had been flipped so the people who were the minority became the majority, or at least a substantial plurality. White was no longer the rule but the exception and getting a job, an education, or a wife was not impossible, but definitely more difficult.

In this essay, I will quickly review some of the stories of my forefathers and chronicle the periods from my birth in 1965 to the present of 2002. During my lifetime, I have had many encounters of racial tension – probably not as harsh as some societal critics may claim after reading this text. I'm sure there are many individuals who can acknowledge far more intense encounters, far more serious profiling and far more abusive situations. But for me, these situations were real, are real, and helped shape the person I am and am becoming. They were not always fair positions to be in. More than once, I was the victim of what is called Reverse Discrimination.

I hope, if anything, these pages allow some discussion to develop about what is fair in the world of racial encounters.

Earliest Encounters

As an infant, my first encounter is slightly beyond my memory but I was told of it as I grew up. It was called the Watts Riot of 1965.

The riot grew out of civil unrest for the status of Black people in the country. Watts was the poorest Black neighborhood in the Los Angeles area and the Negroes were fed up with their station in life.

We lived on the border of Watts, in a city called Lynwood. That night many White people in the area hid in their homes, afraid to go out. My father gathered his guns and laid awake in the living room, ready to protect his home and family should the need arise. Luckily, it did not.

Both my grandparents lived nearby also. My fathers' parents owned a mom and pop grocery store at the corner of Norton and Poplar in Lynwood. We were fortunate that neither any family member, nor the business suffered unduly during the night of duress. Still, the incident prompted my parents to move several cities away to another LA suburb called Downey. My grandparents stayed in Lynwood for a long time afterward, till they were one of the last White families in the city.

Downey was a White city. The people were White. The streets were well maintained. There were a bevy of parks and churches. Even the cops were White. We never had the nicest home on the street, usually affording a decent house in a bad location. We were always on an alley or right up against a freeway, but still it was what was called 'A Good Neighborhood'.

My next encounter as a child was with Maria. She was an illegal immigrant who somehow my parents had come to know. They employed her as a maid in the late sixties to help my mom take care of the house and us kids; my sister, brother and me. I scarcely remember her; except for sometimes eating her cooking or the shadow of a darker lady in the house tending to the kitchen. But, I'm told that I could speak Spanish before I could even speak English. A skill I wish I still had today. Maria would take care of me speaking in her native tongue and I learned to follow her instructions as a child would. Without any hesitation, I followed the instructions of my primary caregiver and eventually learned to respond to her in the language of my upbringing.

These days, my Spanish is deplorable Not only because of the head start I was given as a child, but because I furthered my education of Espanol in Junior High and High school. And while I was quick to pick it up during class, I was also quick to forget it as an adult.

Maria ended up leaving our family's employ when she married my Uncle Edmond, who worked for NASA as an engineer in the 1970's on projects he, at the time, refused to talk about. In later years, he opened up and told us that the projects were the Space Shuttle and the Stealth Bomber.

Stories from my Dad - Before I was born

In the early 1960's, my dad was a Postal carrier. He remembers when the first women were allowed to work in the back room, doing the sorting. Until this time, the women were only working the front counter, but word had come down from the top that women were to receive equal pay as men and they had to have equal work.

Unfortunately for the first woman, who was promoted, the man assigned to work alongside her was not happy with the arrangement and they had to work in a small cramped space. To emphasize his unhappiness he would say to the woman, "Well, if you're gonna do a mans job and earn a mans' pay, then you outta be able to smell a mans fart." After which he would rip the most rancid act of flatulence he could.

It was not a very nice thing for him to do. He was quite large and somewhat unkempt. My father figures it was very unsettling for the woman. But to her credit, she never complained and just kept on working

Elementary School - Downey, CA 1970-1975

My first encounter in Elementary school with a minority was with a woman, or a girl that is. Her name was Katrina Effertz, and I used to chase her around the Kindergarten play yard. She was beautiful, with long blonde hair and long eyelashes. If I wasn't playing blocks or trucks with the boys, I was playing house with Katrina. She would make me be either the Daddy or the baby and I was happy to perform either for her. I believe she left an indelible mark on me, defining the characteristics I would find most attractive in women the rest of my life.

In the fourth grade I got mouthy one afternoon when the boys were acting all tough, being braggarts about their physical capabilities. Some were saying they weren't afraid of anything. Some were saying *anyone*. Me, I chose to be more specific and claimed there wasn't anyone in the schoolyard I wouldn't fight if I had to.

A fellow playmate asked, "Even Marcos?"

"Even Marcos," I said.

Marcos was the biggest kid in the fourth grade; a Mexican boy with the best physical attributes a kid his age could have. He could outrun, out kick, out fight anyone in the schoolyard. Somehow he got wind of my braggadocio remark and took it as a personal challenge. He caught me off guard in a lonely corner of the schoolyard with three or four of my playmates around, who coincidentally had heard my initial claim of being willing to fight anyone.

Marcos said something like, "I heard you want to fight me."

"No," I responded, trying to eyeball my surrounding friends without losing sight of Marcos. "What I said was, if I had to fight you, I wouldn't run."

"So, you want to fight me then," said Marcos, not quite accepting the distinction between the two comments I was trying to make. He balled his fists and improved his stance.

"No," I repeated, my voice rising and octave, "what I meant

was..."

'Whump.' I was hit in the shoulder by Marcos, who didn't wait for any more discussion. "Don't think you can scare me," Marcos threatened. "Or the next time I'll beat you up bad." Then he hit me again square in the chest and the wind was knocked out of my defense. My schoolyard friends left with Marcos to go play kickball.

This incident was not so much an act of racial inequality as it was the simple facts of small kids and big kids interacting on the same playground. For me, I was not influenced by the fact that Marcos was Mexican as much as I learned to not even appear to provoke a fight with a bigger kid. I wonder sometimes, in reflection, if perhaps Marcos was somehow affected or sociologically subconsciously threatened by the fact that he was one of the only Hispanic kids in the school or maybe I'm just trying to read too much into this. Either way, there was another encounter, with another student in the not too distant future of my Elementary education.

By the fifth grade, I was an exceptional student, getting straight A's in all my studies. So, when a student entered my class who spoke no English, and the school had no English as a Second Language program, I was selected to spend extra time with the Latino kid. We primarily spent our time going through a children's Spanish/English dictionary, one with lots of pictures. We started with simple objects and said words like ball, cat, dog, and teacher. It was slow going but I figured I was this kid's introduction to the language and to the country. I wanted to make a good impression on both him and my teacher so I took the work seriously.

Within a few days, the kid had enough English so he could play some sports with us on the playground and he began to get along. But one day, he was simply no longer in the class, a week later I saw him in the special education class of the school with the retarded kids. Soon thereafter, I forgot about him.

At home, my father would bring home stories of work and share them at the dinner table. I always admired my father and his work ethic. He seemed to work hard and that was a quality I tried to emulate in my own life.

He was the manager of Grocery stores for American Markets, who owned the Lucky stores supermarkets, back when supermarkets were a new phrase. I found out later he was a kind of hatchet man sent to stores that needed shaping up, which usually meant the firing of personnel who were poor performers or didn't follow the traditional company policies.

He'd been transferred from one store to another, starting with the Downey store where we lived, in a mostly white neighborhood, to the Whittier store, in a mixed Hispanic/White neighborhood, to the East Los Angeles store, which is a strictly Hispanic neighborhood. I heard my fathers' stories of work, around the dinner table, evolve into discussions of race.

While working at the Whittier store, he would describe the men, and few women, to my mother over dinner. This would often include comments like: "Renee, the Mexican checker," or "George, the black janitor," and then some reference to the quality of their work or their ability to show up on time. Sometimes it would involve a description of the employee bringing their home problems to work. For example: kids who were in need of daycare and parents with no where to leave them.

Not all the references were negative though. One assistant manager, Jerry, was a favorite friend of my family. My Dad even recommended him for advancement to General Manager, which Jerry eventually got. What I remember most about Jerry is how pretty his daughters were, of which he had several. As I got older, I commented on this several times and was always glad when Jerry would bring his family over for visits.

There were also references to white employees. Or at least I assumed the employees referred to without the addendum of race co-notated to their titles and names were white. The comments associated with these employees would be either positive or negative but I don't remember their impact nearly as much as I remember the racial comments.

Again, I don't think my parents were racist as much as it was a new era in social understanding and people were searching for appropriate ways to discuss subjects never addressed in their pasts. There were times individuals were grouped together with statements like, "those people," or "they're all like that," but those were more slips of the tongue than the standard response.

Still I heard them.

When my Dad was transferred to the East Los Angeles store, the stories got worse. East Los Angeles is what could be called a barrio. It was and still is home to the largest population of Spanish speaking people in Southern California. My Dad was the White boss, the Man, and many people hated him for it.

He was sent in to transform a store suffering from mass theft into a profitable location. The dinner table stories became more severe. A few of the more recollectable are:

A black woman is shoplifting watermelons by placing them under her enormous girth, under her dress and holding them between her knees as she tries to waddle out the front door.

A Hispanic woman catches one of her many children stealing candy from the open bins and slaps his hand as the child begins to stuff his mouth. The mother then says," Haven't I told you before? If you're going to steal make sure you get enough for your sisters."

Night crew employees were stealing so much on the late shift they used store carts to bring the merchandise out to their cars. Dad caught these employees by spending the night with one of his assistants in a graveyard across the street, peering into the parking lot through a pair of binoculars.

One of these times my Dad fired a male employee who was part of a gang. Several of his friends showed up and threatened one of the assistants to rehire the man. When the assistant said he couldn't do it without my Dad's approval, and that was unlikely. The large glass windows at the front of the store were blown out that afternoon by a drive-by shooting.

My Dad also went through several cars during these times, mainly due to sugar being fed into the gas tank and tire slashings.

By the end of the Fifth grade, I had one other minority

encounter of my own. My school had the first black student enroll about a month before summer vacation. A black boy in my grade, but not my class, and his little sister a few grades my younger. I had seldom seen a black person up close. It created a confusing feeling in me. As far as I had been told growing up, at least as far as my grandmother, aunts and uncles, black people symbolized a lesser society. I wondered if a black kid in the neighborhood meant we were slipping socially. But these were the thoughts of a child and I knew this even then. The black kid behaved just like anybody else in the school. He was comparable to everyone else in the games we all played. No better, no worse. I began to question if my grandmother was right.

I didn't get long to wonder though. Summer vacation came and I was shipped off to my Grandparents, who'd moved to a small farming community called Madera, outside of Fresno, in North Central California. The hot summer days were spent horseback riding, visiting the Sierra redwoods, fishing and swimming in the San Joaquin River and riding in my Uncle's logging truck.

When I flew back to Los Angeles, my parents picked me up at LAX and drove along the freeway home. When they passed the off ramp leading to our home, I said, "Hey, where are you going? Our house is back there!"

"Oh didn't we tell you," my mother said. "We moved this summer. We now live in a city called Banning about an hour and a half out in the country. Don't worry you'll like it."

My parents went on to tell me they were tired of the hustle bustle of Los Angeles and wanted to live in more open space, away from all the people. But occasionally, there were subtle hints that some of the people they were trying to escape was the exploding minority populations in areas of Los Angeles we could afford to live in. I never thought of my parents as really racists, and I still don't. I just think it was they way of the times.

If they did secretly harbor thoughts of removing us from the racial influx of our former neighborhoods, my parents only succeeded to take my sister, brother and myself out of the frying pan and into the fire.

Grade Six-Junior High, Banning, CA 1976

Banning was supposed to be a fresh start for the family. A rural community an hour and half from Los Angeles, it offered large open spaces, lots of farmland, and room to grow. My brother and I spent many afternoons shooting guns, going hunting and hiking in the nearby hills.

When school started, my mom took my brother and I to buy school clothes. We bought the same clothes we always had. Little did we know the impact that our fashion choice would have on our new schoolmates. We chose the best Hawaiian prints and brand new Levi's our parents' budget could afford and wandered into our new school, Susan B. Coombs Junior High.

Not too far onto campus, as we walked to our first classes, two black boys confronted us, saying, "what are you a couple of Surfer boys?"

"I surfed once, but I'm not really a surfer," I said.

"Shut up," said my brother.

One of them grabbed my collar, wrinkling it, "where'd you get this, the beach?"

I stood my ground but didn't respond. Neither did my brother.

The black boys called us "pussies" and laughed as they walked away.

My family didn't realize until too late that Banning was comprised of 20% black, 30% Mexican, 10% Asian and 40% white. While the white population had the largest majority, they were never more than a substantial plurality in the make up of the area. The schools were a reflection of that diversity. My homeroom class was the epicenter of my day. There were two fat black girls who dominated the class through the sheer volume of their voices. Because of my reddish blonde hair and freckles they nicknamed me Strawberry.

I was small for my age and as Strawberry, I was picked on constantly. There was this one large Mexican girl who made a special purpose of causing me grief. I forget her name, but she liked to trip me in the halls, push me into lockers, anything she could to embarrass me. Being a boy, I was helpless to fight her. I couldn't hit a girl. But she was frightening strong, a good foot taller than me. What's more, I didn't know what I'd done to provoke her in the first place. I was simply the victim of her anger.

Finally, one day, I'd had enough. After she pushed me down in a busy hall between classes, into the lockers, knocking my supplies and books onto the ground, she grabbed all my pencils, threaded them through her fingers and cracked them against her knee, causing them to break in two. Then she tossed them at me and laughed. I was fed up. She'd been doing this for weeks and I knew I couldn't keep living like this. So as she turned away, I called, "hey!" When she turned back around I jabbed a roundhouse punch to the jaw and laid her out.

For my indiscretion, I was sent to the principles office and then suspended for two days. I don't know if anything happened to her. But when I got back to my homeroom class, the black girls congratulated me and treated me like I did well. Apparently the Mexican girl had been tormenting a lot of others also and I'd made a few friends with my misdeed. I returned a sort of conquering hero but was still inwardly ashamed for hitting a girl. Although i was glad she left me alone after that.

But my encounters were not over. Getting rid of one bully sometimes only invites another. By defending myself against a girl, I had brought notoriety to myself. Now, I found myself being confronted by extortionists who wanted my lunch money. An athletic black boy had decided to make me his personal bank account, threatening me with a beating if I didn't give him cash every day. This went on for about two weeks before I figured out a solution.

Fighting this guy was out of the question. As I mentioned earlier, I was smaller than average and he was physically fit. So, I outsmarted him by pitting one bully against another. This time, when he came to me and asked for my lunch money, I pointed to the largest, meanest black guy on campus and said, "I would, but he already took it." The lunch money bully didn't know how to respond and he left me alone from then after.

There was another encounter, that was memorable, although at least I wasn't made to fight or lie. This incident involved another black kid who was in my same class. We had P.E. together and at this time boys were still made to shower in the locker room before going on to their next class. Well, this kid had the largest penis I had ever seen to the day. Possibly still. It was huge and he liked to grab it and shake it as he walked around the locker room. He'd say things too. Things like, "hey, how'd your sister likes one of these?" And "I screwed your momma and she liked it." He was rude and vulgar. But from then on, whenever someone made a reference to the size of black men's penises I always thought of him.

A minor incident I remember happened after I watched a Happy Days episode where a cousin of Fonzi's though he wasn't good at anything until the Fonz discovered his cousin had fast hands and he went for the world record of flipping coins off his elbow and catching the coins in his hand.

I found, by practicing at home, that I was good at the same elbow flipping coin catching trick as Fonzi's cousin and the next day at school I wanted to show off my new trick to my friends.

One of the black kids said, "Go ahead but if they fall on the ground, I'm taking them."

I lined up thirty coins on my elbow and did the flip. I only caught a few. The coins sprayed onto the ground and the kids scrambled for them like candy from a piñata.

There was a positive occurrence in my year of Junior High in Banning.

During the spring, the school held a Spelling Bee. We had to face a homeroom written test first, and then there was buildings face off in front of a few select teachers, and then the finalists had a showdown in front of the entire school in the auditorium. There must have been a thousand kids watching and I was my building champion. When it got down to me and another kid, one of the black girls yelled,

"Go Strawberry," and the entire audience burst out laughing.

My opponent was given the word Xylophone and missed. I got the word right and won. Back in my homeroom the next day I was amazed at the reaction of many of the kids. Especially by those who were some of the worst spellers, who were coincidentally black. They talked about the Spelling Bee as if they were on the stage with me, As if by being in the same class somehow allowed us to share in the victory. I guess in some ways it did. Much like an Olympian adds glory to his hometown, as Spelling Bee champ I made those kids who suffered miserably from poor literacy share in a little bit of intellect. It was strange but true at the same time.

The only other thing of note, I remember was one day in P.E. class a kid was swinging on the chin-up bars trying to do one more pull-up when his leg fell off. I didn't know it until I saw it, but the kid had a false leg, a prosthetic, and as he struggled to pull-up one more time, the bindings came loose and off fell his leg. He was embarrassed. And it answered for me the question of why he always wore long pants to P.E., even in hot weather.

My parents moved from Banning after only one year. Apparently, while I was having difficulties of my own adjusting to my schoolmates, my sister was having even more troublesome times dealing with being a freshman new-meat white girl at Banning High School. The Mexican boys were scaring her into dating them and she was scared not to. That summer we moved to Palm Springs, once more hoping to escape the racial problems. In some ways we did. But in others we were not so fortunate.

Grade Seven-Junior High, Palm Springs 1976-79

Palm Springs had a catch phrase attached to its name at the time we moved there. It was called 'the home of the newly wed and the nearly dead'. There was even a hillside development called 'Cardiac Hill'. But all that was OK by us. We thought we were moving up in the world just to be moving there.

What we didn't know, was that Palm Springs was no longer quite the celebrity haven it had the reputation of being. Its glorious past was gone and what was left was a bunch of rich wanna-be's and hanger-onners who had little respect for the new working class families moving into the area. The old-timers didn't want development. Jobs were scarce and activities for the youth were unheard of.

Plus the treatment of minorities was abhorrent. As little as a decade earlier, an entire area of the city known as section 14 had been cleared of all the black residents and moved into an area north of town called the Gateway neighborhood, or simply the North end. This end was forcibly achieved through a series of city delivered eviction notices and bulldozing of homes. There were also a pocket of poor black homes directly across the golf course from where our small condo was that the realtor conveniently neglected to tell my parents about. It's called the Crossley tract, after the main street running into it.

There were several such neighborhoods scattered throughout the desert. Blacks generally kept to Black neighborhoods and Mexicans kept to Mexican neighborhoods. These factors combined to create a few encounters for me once I got settled in.

The first friend I made in Palm Springs was a Jewish boy named Cory. Cory had, at the time, the unfortunate coincidence of looking a lot like Sylvester Stallone. Coupled with the fact that Cory had an East coast accent, made him the subject of pre-teen ridicule, particularly, because of his being undeservingly picked on, Cory went to extensive effort to turn his weakling frame into pure muscle and also trained in boxing and fighting. Later in life, Cory's resemblance to the Action superstar would result in him meeting women with ease.

By the time he was in High School, Cory was force to be reckoned with and nobody dared pick on him. But that took a few years of hard work. I've always admired Cory for putting up with the pubescent cruel crap that some kids can dish out and making the determination to commit to a lengthy project of self-improvement. Once he told me the real turning point was when he went to his dad for sympathy and was told, "If you don't go out there and kick the biggest bully of the bunch's ass, then when you get home I'm going to kick yours."

Fearing for his safety from his dad, Cory went out that week and fought the biggest bully he could and the turning point in his life began.

The second friend I made was with a girl named Cricket. I'm

not sure if Cricket was Malado or Mexican or what. She had dark olive skin and curly black/brown hair. She wore not the best clothes and bore a chip on her shoulder the size of a school bus. As I was skinny, short kid, there were several times that Crickets mouth defended me against school bullies in the beginning days of my Junior High life. She also introduced me to group of kids called the Fielders. Together we'd go and jump the fence at the end of the playground and lay in a vacant field to smoke cigarettes and bad-talk the teachers.

Cricket never finished school with me. She was eventually expelled from regular school and had to attend Continuation school; which is where all the bad kids have to go. I don't think she ever finished Continuation school either. Several times through Junior High and High school she appeared on campus for a month or a year but she never lasted. Finally I lost track of her in my junior year of High school and didn't meet her again until I was in my late twenties. We never let ourselves lose our friendship again.

My brother and I rode the same bus to school. It was one of

those great big double rowed buses that held some 100 or more passengers and would pick us up, with about a dozen other kids in a 5 block area and then head directly to C Street. C Street was a Mexican neighborhood in nearby Cathedral City.

I remember the bus would pull up the first stop on C Street, there were only two, and approximately 50 kids would be waiting in front of a large Catholic church with huge stained glass windows and extensive architecture.

They'd come onto the bus and fill it up; being loud mouths, speaking Spanish and giving the white kids dirty looks. If it wasn't for my brother and a half dozen white boys, of which my brother Darrell was one, and who were the best fighters on the bus, we'd have gotten our butts kicked every day. But because of these boys who kept the peace for the rest of us, we held the back seat seats of the bus. The back seats were the most coveted because they were the furthest away form the bust driver, allowing us to get away with making the most noise and any other bit of rule breaking we wanted to get away with.

My Brother was known as a bad ass on campus. He could fight

with the best of them and he often did. He had two best friends named Dean and Philip, and the three of them caused enough trouble to keep them on a first name basis with the Vice-Principal, because they were constantly being sent to his office.

They'd get into a fight with someone for simple reasons like a misspoken statement, a crossed look or sometimes just the unfortunate mistake of looking too much like a geek. At times Darrell, Dean and Philip were just cruel. Their troublesome ways had repercussions like ripples in a pond. They would protect you if they were around, but they weren't always around.

One time, just outside of woodshop, I was sitting on the ground with my back up against a wall doing some homework. I had gotten my woodshop project done and asked the teacher if I could step outside and do the work so I could get away from the sound of the table saws.

While minding my own business, this one tall lanky black basketball center, named Tee, came across me there and stood over me. "Looky what I found me?" He said. There were gangs growing up in the desert. The blacks had formed themselves into a group called the blue coats. They all wore blue parkas even in the warm spring months. Tee was their leader.

"What?" I said forgetting my homework to see who was talking to me and not liking the sneer on Tee's face.

"Where's you brother now?" Tee said and he slapped my head.

"Hey, leave me alone," I said. " I haven't done nothing."

Tee answered, "Like I fucking care," and then he started kicking me. He kicked me more times than I could count. I tried to deflect the first couple thinking he would stop, or someone would come by and stop him. No one came by and he didn't stop till I was crumpled on the ground in a ball, crying. Then he gave me a couple more kicks. Finally he left me balling on the sidewalk with my homework scattered all around.

The bell rang, signaling I should go to my next class. Kids swirled out classroom doors. I picked myself up, wiped away tears with a now dirty sleeve and never told anyone. I was too embarrassed.

The same thing happened to Philips younger brother William,

only worse. Four or five black kids cornered William and beat him up so bad they broke his arm. It was the worst case of gang fighting that the school had seen; one boy beaten badly by a group of thugs.

What made things worse was that William and Philip had a slew of older brothers in their late teens and twenties. The kind of stories when people talk of families going after families began to seem more than rumor. William and Philip were known as dirty fighters and their brothers had even worse reputations. Some of the brothers had been to Juvenile Hall, or prison, and they were known to carry weapons. Plus, there father was said to be in the Hells Angels.

Philip took on several of the black kids at once himself and was beaten up. He lost the fight but half the black kids he fought had bruises and fat lips. Still, word had it that the fight had been the result of the blacks stalking Philip, looking for an opportunity to take him out. Philips brothers and father were now upset and wanting to help.

Within a few days there was tale of the Hells Angels coming to our Junior High to even the score. Tensions were high and police patrolled the perimeter of campus. The air around school was thick with predictions and then by the time a week had passed and everyone was settling down, it happened.

It was the end of the school day and all the kids were loading onto buses to head home. I was already in my seat at the back of the bus when I heard the rumble of a long line of Harley Davidson motorcycles. I stood in my seat to look out the window and rounding the corner of the school buildings was something I had only heard of in the news before; a full contingent of Hells Angels riding their infamous Harleys, clad in leather and Levi's, ready to even the score.

There were only about twenty bikers, but they made a noise like a thousand hoof beats. Following them was a white Cadillac like chariot throne of an emperor drawn by stampeding horses. I immediately turned to check out the bus which normally went to the North end into the Gateway neighborhood. Black boys and girls were pouring out of it from every window and doorway. Not waiting for an easy exit, they were opening emergency hatches, climbing out and running. One climbed into my bus and hid at my feet, trying to crawl under the seat.

"What 're you doing?" I asked.

44

"Hidin' fool," he said, still trying act tough.

"Who you calling fool, fool," I yelled. "Hey, we got one hiding over here!" I jumped up and pointed at him, making big gestures so nobody would miss him.

"Fuck," he said and crawled out the window.

The police were on the scene fast. No actual fighting happened, but a stand was definitely made. The Hells Angels had come to defend some of their sons who had been mistreated and this was not to happen again. For the rest of that year not a blue coat was seen on campus. William and Philip were both expelled from school and permanently sent to Continuation.

Darrell and Dean ended up in Continuation also before the end of the year when the decided to fight a history teacher they though was a jerk. It was a stupid thing to do, but they did it just the same. The end result was the teacher was a better fighter than they thought. They lost the fight, Dean's parents moved him away to San Jose and Darrell never went to regular school again.

I finished up the school year living off the reputation of my brother; I didn't need protection because of the happenings earlier in the year.

In between the fights, I was in class. On day, in third period science class I received a flyer outlining an essay competition on the subject, "Why I'm proud to be an American." There was a group of four of us sitting together when the flyer was dropped off. There was one pretty Mexican girl, Tracy Milward, who sat near me and to impress her, I began reciting what I would write if I were to enter the competition. She liked what she heard and starting writing to my dictation.

The result was a quickly finished competition length essay that we put both our names on and dropped off to the teacher with the flyer. By the end of school we were informed that we'd won the school, city and county levels, and we had to declare only one of us as the true author to go on to the state finals. I told Tracy that she could go to Sacramento and try and win.

She did. But, when forced to sit and write another essay on the spot as part of the competition she failed. I always wondered if I were to have gone could I have done better. The essay was largely my thoughts. Tracy had only injected a few sayings. Perhaps I would have. Perhaps I would have choked. I'll never know.

Summer is a long time to a kid, the three months away from peers can cleanse you. In my case, it wiped the slate clean with many of the enemies of the previous year. I also got my first real job that summer. I got hired onto the Chart House restaurant as a dishwasher.

The Chart House was a good place to work. It had a bevy of young people working there and I was glad to be one of them. The hours were long and the shifts were hard. But, they were also fun. I worked about 4-5 days a week including school days and often got off at 3 AM and had to be at school by 7:30. Fortunately, the Child Labor Laws were a new thing and not strictly enforced.

After I was trained, I soon rose to the position of senior dishwasher, mainly because I was too young and small to be promoted to anything else. But, about six months into my employment I was given a Mexican man named Martin (Marteen) to train.

Martin was approximately 40 years old and didn't speak any English. I had taken Spanish classes at school the semester before enabling me to speak to Martin in a broken manner.

At first, Martin was anxious to learn the job. He worked hard and tirelessly. Within a few weeks, he brought his brother-in-law Rudolfo to work with him and I was training him also. Within a few months Martin and Rudolfo were able to work all the shifts, without a break, and I came to the realization that I had trained my replacements. But soon thereafter Martins work ethics began to fade. He came in drunk and complained often. He was rude to the waiters and sexually harassed the waitresses. Finally, his employment was terminated one night when he came into work so drunk he could barely stand.

Rudolfo on the other hand was an excellent employee. With Martin gone he really came into his own. He worked the nights as dishwasher and then took on day jobs around the restaurant also like clean-up, prep cooking and gardening. And he brought other members of his family north from Mexico to fill as many positions as the restaurant would hire. Within a few years, he had six or seven family members working under him and had all support positions filled.

One thing about Rudolfo though. He and his wife Maria kept having children. They had up to eight girls during the nine years I worked at the Chart House. He always wanted a boy though and it never seemed to come. Just before I left for another career, which we'll get to later, he had his son and Rudolfo and Maria quit having kids.

Later in life, I ran into Rudolfo and Maria and thought they must have really done something right. There was a time we both did the same job, side by side and yet twenty years later he had retired to what seemed a comfortable life and I was still working hard.

Training Rudolfo filled my summer between seventh and Eighth grade. I went back to school feeling a little more of a man because I now had my own income. The oldest and meanest Blue coats had graduated and gone onto High school, leaving behind the ones who weren't as aggressive. On the school bus though, all hell was about to break loose.

It was the final year of Junior High School, eighth grade, and all the big boys had either moved onto High school or C School, leaving just me and some other short white boys, not known for being fighters, behind to defend ourselves.

Our situation was never really discussed openly. But for some reason when the school bus came to our stop and we loaded on, we all sat around the front seats, staying close to the driver and leaving the back seats of the bus available for all the Mexican kids.

When the bus came to the stop by the Catholic church, the Mexican kids loaded into the bus making all sorts of noise as usual. When they saw the back seats of the bus waiting wide open for them, there was only the briefest of pauses and then they clamored for the prime positions. One Mexican boy, named Hector, had also risen from one of the younger boys in his group to being the oldest in his own Junior High gang. He and his friends claimed the back seat as their own new domain.

There was a second bus stop in the barrio. At that location, only a few passengers loaded on, and this year there was a single pretty white girl wearing her best skirt who was in the group. Her name was Kristi and she seemed out of place getting on the bus in this neighborhood. Obviously her parents were not very well off, or else she would live in a different neighborhood. She was wearing a white skirt with tiny red hearts on it, and a red sweater. There were clean but cheap clothes. She had worn her best for the first day of school. I was taken with her from the first day I saw her, but I was shy and she was prettier than anyone I had ever tried to impress, so I stayed in my seat and let the other kids talk to her.

Hector was taken with her too. Within days he was grabbing her as she got off the bus. The bus route was reversed in the afternoons so Kristi would get off first. Hector would position his seat so Kristi would have to pass her to get off the bus. The first time or two she was caught off guard. We all were. Kristi would be shocked, embarrassed and then run off the bus. Hector would laugh like the bully he was, exclaim loudly in Spanish as he welcomed jeers and applause from his friends. Then he'd join them at the back of the bus, like a warrior returning to his clan.

These actions inspired the other Mexican kids to pick on the white kids in other ways. The Mexican girls would talk about the White girls in Spanish right in front of them. The white girls of course didn't know what was being said, but when being stared down and talked about in a foreign language they started getting the point. The Mexican girls would talk and laugh and point and when a white girl would stare back, the Mexican girl would get confrontational and say something like, "What are you staring at, bitch."

Being outnumbered and unsure, the white girl would respond, "Uh, nothing."

"Uh, Nothing," the Mexican girl would mock. "I didn't think so. You better just watch out, Pinche Cabrone. Or I'll knock you upside the head." Then they'd go back to talking in Spanish, with even more fierce looks on their faces.

The challenges grew even more obnoxious; white kid's books were getting knocked out of their hands; spit wads shot at their heads; girl's hair being pulled. We were all pretty scared of our twice a day bus ride. The bus driver would protect us when things got totally out of control but that left a lot of room for abuse. And sometimes he didn't always catch it, and sometimes he just got tired of being the policeman and let it ride.

Meanwhile, Hector had increased his tormenting of Kristi. He was positioning himself for both her morning boarding and her afternoon unloading. He was grabbing her hair, standing in her way so she had to squeeze past him and he could push his groin into her, or even going for a full feel of her breast. He was becoming quite the terror on the bus too. Anyone who even looked at him while he did this got a head slap or a punch. Hector was the kingpin on the bus. For weeks his domination of the bus riders grew through intimidation, coercion and fear of his fists and his gang.

His power climaxed when one morning, as Kristi loaded onto the bus. She was wearing her favorite white dress with the tiny red hearts and Hector was positioned to get his feel. She shied away from having to pass him but there weren't any vacant seats available until after him. His friends had also taken up seats near him, instead of the back, so something was planned. She tried to rush past but he was quicker; this time he didn't just settle for a little feel or forcing her to squeeze past. This time he reached down below the hem of her dress and ran his hands all the way up her legs and kept feeling all the way up over her chest. He drew her dress all the way to her shoulders, leaving her panties and bare legs exposed for everyone to see.

I couldn't stand it any more. We White kids had been tormented too long. Kristi had definitely taken more than anyone deserved to take. I had sat in my seat far too long and let the bullies take over what was once a good fun time of a bus ride and even though I wasn't a very good fighter by any standard, on the spur of the moment, seeing Kristi screaming in terror, I decided to risk it all.

Without thinking, I flew over the seat and grabbed Hector in a head lock before he knew what was going on. I punched him in the face one-two then three times in rapid succession. Momentarily, I was afraid his gang friends would attack me simultaneously, but they all were taken off guard. Then I slammed Hectors face into the metal rail on the back of seat two times and let him fall.

Hector was not able to stand. He grabbed his face and cried.

The bus driver had shouted, "Hey!" As I was hitting Hector but the fight flashed by before he got in a second word.

After I let Hector go I shouted to all the White Kids, "Come on, Let's take the back of the bus!" And all the White kids left their seats and stormed to the rear of the bus. We boys took the very back seat and all the girls sat around us, even Kristi, as one of the girls from our bus stop soothed her hurt ego.

Hector was regaining his senses and some his gang had stood up to take action.

The bus driver shouted again, "you, off the bus."

"Hey man, we didn't do nothing," said Hector's second in command.

"I saw what happened," said the bus driver, "I want you off the bus now and you're not riding again for week."

Hector and his friends spat curses in Spanish, but they left the bus. The dark spell of the Mexican bullies was broken. The remaining Mexican kids who were still bullies and hadn't been caught in the fracas remained furiously silent. But, even their evil glares were less menacing.

There was some good fallout from the fight. It seems that

Hector and his gang were also restraining the good intentions of many of the Mexican kids. Nearly all of those kids who stayed on the bus became friendly with us from the White neighborhood. It was like a great big sigh of relief had escaped during the fight. Some of those Mexican kids who stayed on the bus were friends of mine all the way through High school. One of them, Arnold, was one of the funniest guys to have around.

A week later, Kristi invited me over to her house to play. I was dumbstruck, but did my best to act cool when I agreed. Her house was a run down plank building that had gone decades without a paint job. She'd cleaned it up as best she could and we ate ice cream on the porch steps. She wore a blue dress this day and looked absolutely stunning. After the ice cream she made some effort to sit close. I missed my opportunity for a kiss on the mouth, I don't know exactly how I could have done better, but I'm sure a more suave guy could have gotten at least a kiss of gratitude from her. But, I was shy and hadn't ever kissed anyone like that before. So, I missed my chance. She did give me a peck on the cheek before I left. I caught the public city bus and rode home.

Hector made another stand against me a few weeks later. I was out of class, during a period, on my way to the library when I passed Hector and his gang smoking cigarettes in the hall. He shouted at me, "you want some now, Hoto."

"Any time, any where asshole," I answered, stopping in the hall to square off at him. I was very scared but figured if I ran or backed down it would be his cue to go on the warpath again.

Hector spat more curses in Spanish, all his friends laughed at me, but not one of them left the wall to advance a fight. I let them have their dirty words and went on the library. Hector and I never confronted each again.

There was only one other minor incident in Junior High school. It was one of my dating mistakes in life. Sue Collins asked me to go to the Sadie Hawkins dance and I said yes; that wasn't the mistake. The mistake was a few days later, when Patti Axelrod asked to go and I said yes again.

Patti was the girl I wanted to go with most, but Sue had asked a week before and rather than end up dateless I said yes thinking that Patti would never ask. I was wrong. When Patti finally did ask I couldn't help but want to go. But, after I said Yes, I knew that I had seriously goofed. With only two days till the dance, I turned to Cricket for advice.

Cricket called me an idiot, which I was. But, she also knew how to fix it. She convinced me that the right thing to do was to go with Sue to the dance and then went of to tell Patti about a rumor she'd heard that I had two dates to Sadie Hawkins. Before an hour had passed Patti confronted me in the halls and asked if the rumor was true.

I said it was and was extremely embarrassed. Patti totally understood and acted as if Sue had merely beaten her to the prize. I'd got off easy, although Patti did tell me something about Sue that never got out of my head.

"You know she's bald," Patti said.

"No way," I replied.

"Yeah," Patti corrected. "Sue wears a wig. Her hair is fake."

Then Patti turned and walked away, "have fun."

On the date, I dressed in Levi's and a plaid shirt and rented a limousine to pick up Sue. The car pulled up to her house and I went to the door carrying a small bouquet of flowers, which she took, tossed inside her house and ran to the limo. I followed her and we talked and laughed the whole way to the dance.

At the dance, we had a great time. The gymnasium had been decorated like the inside of a barn with lots of hay bells and home signs saying things like "Watering Hole" and "Photograffey." We danced almost every song, except for when we stopped to drink, eat or get our picture taken. It was a swell time.

When the dance ended, we rode home in the limo. I was really embarrassed and never a made a move on her. We just sat on separate ends of the same bench seat in this great big car and rode home. She got out and I finally made a move for a kiss but it was too little too late. Sue didn't even want to kiss by then and she stormed into her house.

On the way to mine, the driver kept looking at me in the rearview mirror. I didn't have anything to say. I knew I'd missed another opportunity with a girl and I didn't know when I'd get another chance. I felt like a loser.

To further lesson my self-esteem, when I got home I didn't have any money left to tip the driver. He got out, opened my door to let me out and I walked right past him with his hand out, past my mom who was watching me from the front door and went into my room.

The driver shouted something, which I heard but couldn't do anything about, and left in a fit.

So much for my glorious Junior High school days; the remainder of the school year finished with me being in an arm cast from a motorcycle accident and most of the summer was a bummer. By August though I was all healed up and looking forward to getting away from my younger geeky days. By the time September rolled around, I was looking forward to High school. Growing up, and maybe getting another chance at girls.

Palm Springs High School 1979-1983

High school was to be my break out, my new me, my new identity. To achieve this I created a new persona. I dropped the Hawaiian prints and started wearing a straw cowboy hat, complete with a feather hat band and a roach clip tail. I picked up an attitude too, although I didn't deserve it. I was till the same wimpy short guy I had always been. I was small for my size, with no signs of any upcoming growth spurts.

It didn't take long before I had my first Minority Encounter. It was at a Pep Rally inside the gym. The whole school had turned out to cheer on the Football team in the first game of the year. The bleachers were divided into four sections so the seniors sat with the seniors, the juniors with the juniors and so on. I sat down near the front of the freshman section.

During one of the "We've got Spirit, Yes we do," chants, something struck me in the back of the head. I turned and no one or nothing seemed to be the culprit. "We've got Spirit, How about You?" Something hit me again. This time a wad of paper fell to my side.

I turned to face the crowded stands. No one stood out to me. Just a sea of chanting faces. "Our Spirit is Sky High!" I returned my attention to cheering. Feet stomping became the action called for. Another crumpled paper ball struck me.

"Awe, come on," I turned to the crowd again. No one looked at me. "Stop it," I shouted. Then I stomped my feet some more. The cheerleaders were turning somersaults on the floor and I wanted to watch. But, another paper ball hit my hat. The crowd was roaring now, and I turned to face them. "Whoever is throwing this at me should stop. Fuck you asshole, whoever you are!" I threw the ball up into the stands.

Not long after the Pep Rally ended and I walked out of the

gymnasium. Immediately someone pushed me in the shoulder. I stumbled. Caught myself and turned around prepared to fight.

There was a Mexican boy my same age standing there who was ready for me. "What'd you say to me?"

"I didn't say anything to you. I yelled to whoever was throwing those paper balls at me stop and called him an asshole." I didn't even know this guy in front of me. He had a bone to pick with me though.

"Yeah, you called me an asshole," he pushed me again.

"If you're throwing stuff at me," I said. "I guess you are." I tried to hit him and missed.

He was on me instantly. He was a much better fighter and began pummeling me.

I tried to turn it into a wrestling match and failed.

He landed on top of me and began to really dress me up with punches.

But, after the third punch he was knocked off me by one of the football players, Boris King. Boris was the city's best hope at winning trophies. He was one of those streamlined muscled running backs who could move like lightning, and he was black as darkness.

I tried to regain, my hat and my cool. But, Boris thought I was reentering the fight and he knocked me flat. "Both of you stop this shit," he yelled. A crowd had gathered around us, hoping for more. They also slowed down the faculty from making it to the center.

"I didn't start this," I yelled back. "He did."

"I don't care. It ends now."

The Mexican boy said something under his breath and left through his side of the crowd. I put my hat on my head and left also. The teachers made it into the clearing too late to know who or what really happened. No one was punished.

I never knew why the fight happened. I learned my opponents' name, but I soon forgot it. He was transferred to C school with two weeks of school starting. Apparently he was a bad egg that had reached his scrambling. I was just part of his rap sheet.

Boris had a unique life. He was Big Man on Campus all of his High School days. He was always coaches' first pick for Team Captain and Ball carrier. He excelled at both football and Baseball. He even went semi-pro for a while after school. But somewhere after that he reached his peak in athletics and he never made pro. He did marry one of the prettiest White girls on campus, Laurie White; a seeming pun for the blackest, most well known, man at school.

It created a stigma for Laurie though. She was the first girl in my recollection who openly dated a black man. The year was 1980 and this was still a new thing for the world, at least the young world of High School in Palm Springs.

My next encounter was about 12 months later in my sophomore year.

I was out of class for some reason, probably going to the library again. I was always going to the library. I had a real fondness for books and would go there often. Anyways, I had stopped by the soda machines and had just purchased a fresh one. I cracked it open and took a drink.

One of the dirtier, meaner, older black guys on campus appeared in front of me out of nowhere.

"Give me a drink," he said.

There was no one else around. Everyone was in class. I was scared, so I offered up my soda with a shaky hand.

As soon as it was up an inch, He snatched it from me. Then he hocked up a loogey, spit on the top of the can and took a big gulp.

Furor swept over me and I don't know where next move came from.

"Fucking Nigger," I yelled and slapped the can away from him. I poured out a third of the can and wiped the top as I walked away. "Fucking God Dam Asshole Nigger. Take My Fucking Soda." I took a drink and kept walking. I kept waiting for him to punch me in the back of the head and take it back but he never did. I rounded the next corner before I looked back and breathed a sigh of relief when I saw he was no't following me.

I walked a little faster the rest of the way to the library.

There was one more encounter in High school.

In my senior year, I was ahead of my necessary credits to graduate. I had a full day of Radio Broadcasting (KPSH - The Station heard round the block), Office Aide, Woodshop, Band, Swimming (with the Cheerleaders, one of my smartest moves), and Drama. So in my second semester I went ahead and took a bonehead history course. I figured, I like reading and history, so if I take an easy history class, I'll just sit around for an hour and talk interesting subjects with some light reading.

"What I got was a lesson in some of the disparity of education with some of the least intelligent kids in school. 5 star members of the school basketball team were in the class, as were many of the school rejects from all the other history classes. Tee, who had kicked me into a ball in Junior High, was one of the basketball players. There were only two White kids in the class and I was one of them. The other would have flunked auto shop because he couldn't read the manual.

It was disheartening. The textbook was a series of single page reading assignments with a picture on one page and the words on the other, in large print. The really hard part to understand was that all the other kids in the class were having difficulty reading the book. When the teacher would call on them, they'd read like their mouth was a fist full of thumbs. I was surprised to actually see the level of education that until then was only rumors and parental remarks. I had heard of kids like these but I'd never seen them in their own failure.

I thought of transferring out, but the teacher was really kind of a cool guy. He convinced me that I could get the easy A I had thought of in the beginning and I might just be able to help some of these other kids learn something. So I stuck it out.

At first, Tee gave me a hard time. Calling me names and threatening me physically. But, another black kid in the group, named Patrick Henry, stood up for me. It was a simple gesture but it broke the ice. He simply said, "Lay of him, man. Meeks is cool," and Tee did lay off me.

After that, I started lead discussions from my seat. I'd let the minority kids have their say on something and I'd fill in the gaps. Often we laughed and joked about somebody in history. I became fun.

The teacher was lenient during test time, which was only a 10 question quiz at the end of every week. He'd let me whisper to some of the kids in the class if they had a question. I wouldn't always just give up the answer. Sometimes I'd respond with a clue and you'd hear the kid go"Oh yeah." Then they could answer the question.

We'd just have to study a chapter a week. That meant only a single page of reading, with a picture to help. Most of the kids couldn't do it. As I mentioned earlier, it was real eye opener for me, realizing the level of lack of education prevalent in public schooling. But in the end, I was glad I'd stuck it out. Most of those kids got better grades than they had in a long time and I have to think I had something to do with that.

Years later, when I had my first bookstore, I ran a radio ad offering to help anyone in the city with their education if they needed and wanted help. I said, "I can't promise I can help you myself if your education is beyond mine, but if there's any way I can help someone in this city better themselves, I will do anything within my power."

One of the Black kids from that High school history class ought me out. He wanted to be a cop and had failed the entrance exam a couple of times. I sympathized with him and told him I'd see what I could do. He showed me some of his writing and it was poor. He also explained that he had trouble describing a series of events at a crime scene because he'd get the timing all screwed up.

I showed him how by using all capital letters he neatens up his printing. I also showed him how to draw a time line complete with legs to illustrate significant events.

He said he'd never seen a timeline before but understood it immediately. He thought it would help him to clarify the sequence of events before he tried to write them in a report and he thanked me.

He went off to take the test again but never became a cop. He did volunteer for a number of years though and they let him wear a uniform and drive the patrol car. I would see him directing traffic before church at the largest congregation in town. I'm sure it gave him a feeling of significance and servitude. He always had a smile on his face as he waved me through. I still like him and enjoy seeing him from time to time.

During my senior year of High school, a long time friend of mine showed homosexual tendencies. It was a time when men were wearing neon green or pink Polo shirts but he seemed to go the extra mile and even gained a swish in his walk. It was all the talk of the other guys on campus, especially once he made a friend. We'll call him W. The two were best friends. No one ever saw them kiss that I heard of, but it seemed obvious that the two were taken with each other. They were inseparable, although if I had to guess I'd say W was the top. But, who knows.

College of the Desert - 1984-1987

College was a time of great fun. It was a time of finding me in my studies, growing beyond my parents' control, and a time of discovering my first true love.

Her name was Teresa. We were on the school newspaper together. She was the top reporter and I was the managing editor. My best friend, Dan, was the Editor-in-Chief. We conquered all sorts of seemingly important topics of the day: School Budget cuts, teacher understaffing, closed down a Board of Trustees meeting for violating the Brown act, and even got the Dean to retire early because of intensive coverage of unfair administrative pay raises. It was a wonderful time. We worked long hours on the paper and let our regular studies suffer. We loved it.

I was also on the Student Council, as Student Trustee, to the

Board of Trustees. During one of the Student Council meetings I had my first Minority Encounter of my College career.

On the Student Council, one of our duties included approving Club Charters. It was in this regard that I got to meet Peaches. Peaches was a robust young Black woman who wanted to start an African American club. She said the purpose of the club was to promote the racial heritage of Black people, to celebrate everything unique about black people, and help them understand their place in culture.

I said, "that sounds great. Can I join?" You must understand that I am about as White as White gets. Peaches was unsure of how to answer.

"Uh, well...I guess," she stammered. "But, why would you want to? This is for Black people."

"I want to understand Black people better," I said. "I want to appreciate their heritage and I never get this kind of information from a classroom. So can I join?"

"I don't know," Peaches said, "But, I'd like to withdraw my application until I think about this some more."

Peaches left that day a little baffled and that was just fine by me. I liked Peaches for her determination and her willingness to create something new, but at the same time I resented the fact that there were no allowances for a White guy club. I mean, if a bunch of white guys wanted to get together and celebrate everything White, we'd be called racists. So why should a bunch of Black people be allowed to get together under the same standard and celebrate everything Black? It was this double standard that provoked me into giving Peaches a hard time.

Peaches did eventually come back to the Student Council for a Charter approval. This time it was for a Rainbow club that would celebrate all sorts of nationalities and races. She was even the impetus that created the first International day at the College. On that day all sorts of nationalities and races created booths and displays to promote their heritage. It was really neat. There were pretty Spanish dancers, Black people with African dress, a German booth, etc., etc.

I still didn't see a White guy booth. But, hey, you can't have it all.

During college, I took a part-time job at the local fish market. It was called the Desert Wharf and I was a very young assistant manager, which meant I was allowed to open and close on Sunday's when the owner would take a day off.

There was a Black cook who had worked there longer than I. His name was Julius and he resented the fact that I got the title assistant manager. He was four years older than me and had worked there on and off for three years. It was the on and of part that kept him from being promoted. Anytime he decided he didn't want to work he simply didn't show up. But he couldn't understand something like determination and responsibility as factors that added up to promotion and increases in pay.

Julius and I had several Minority Encounters.

He liked to call me White Boy when nobody else was around. He's really drag it out too, saying it loud and long, like an inner city slur. When he was especially upset with his station in life he would even call me Honkey.

One Sunday, after he must have had an exceptionally pissy Saturday night, he was more belligerent than usual. Calling me names for hours. Honkey, White Boy, Bitch, Mother Fucker, The Man, all sorts of names flew from his mouth.

Finally, I was tired of his attitude and when the customers cleared out of the store, I threw some names back at him, "Shut your mouth, Nigger. I'm tired of you lip."

"Ooh, hooh. Honkey boss called me a Nigger," Julius laughed. "Yazzir, Mr. man. I'z be quiet now boss." Julius continued to harass me that day, but at a much quieter tone. For some reason he seemed pleased that he'd provoked me into calling him Nigger. As if, there was some reward in that. I didn't understand the reasoning behind that but that's how it was. That's how it always was with Julius, you had to stand up to him to earn his respect.

Another time, I was feeling sick and spent much of my shift in the restroom. When Julius wanted the bathroom and he thought I'd been in there enough, he pounded on the door. He kept pounding until I couldn't help but answer him.

"Get yo ass out of there, White boy," he yelled at me.

"Listen Nigger," I yelled back. "If you're between me and getting out of here when I open that door, I'm left with no choice but to fight you. So Back off."

Again Julius liked this. He told me later that what I'd said made sense to him. After all, there no other way out of the bathroom except for a single door and if he was blocking my way out, then he knew we'd have to fight. So he backed off enough to let me out of the John. Even though Julius could have kicked my butt anytime he wanted to, he was a lean muscular build and had been in many more fights than me, or at least he claimed he had. He also claimed he had a Johnson the size of a horse and had slept with many women. But, who knows.

After a while, Julius and I became more friends than adversaries. He even invited me out with some of his bros. That night, after work, I gave Julius a ride home into an area called the ranch. The Ranch was a four block neighborhood of all black people. It was the closest thing to a slum on the east end of the valley. It was filed with small run-down homes, shopping carts on untended lawns, broken down cars, and chairs out in front of the garages with men drinking beer in the evening.

I was driving my girlfriends four wheel drive Toyota pick-up. It was in really good shape and helped me feel out of place. Julius had told me that tonight we'd smoke some crack. I had never done that before. But thought, 'What the Hey.' I've done other drugs. How weird can it be?

Julius had me pull in front of one of the ranch houses and wait outside. So, I sat there in the Toyota truck, all by myself, and tried not to stare back at the Black people who looked at me like a turd on a turkey, like I didn't belong to be where I was. And they were right. I didn't belong. But, I waited for Julius to return twenty minutes later, with three friends who climbed in the back of he truck, and we headed off to my condo only a few miles away.

At the entrance to the condominium was a guard shack. The guard gave me a look like I was being held hostage and he just needed the High sign to call the cops. I told him everything was fine and he waved us in.

My condo was just a small two bedroom that my girlfriend and I shared in Indio. It was nothing real fancy by my standards, but after just leaving the Ranch, it seemed like a palace. There was white carpeting inside and freshly painted walls. The furniture was neat and in good condition and we had a nice television. I told the guys they had to take their shoes off outside and did so myself. Their hightop tennis shoes proved more difficult than I imagined but hey eventually unlaced them enough to leave them by the door. There was only four pair, but they made a huge pile, and we all went in.

Inside, the contrast between our stations in life continued. The white walls and carpet made the Black guys stand out like spots on a wedding dress. They were the dark in a world full of white. If this is how I felt when we first got in, my senses sharpened after smoking the crack and I became even more obsessed with how things looked.

The crack was small chips of white wrapped in aluminum foil. It was rock cocaine no bigger than some pieces of a cracked marble, or broken glass. One of the guys had a glass pipe to smoke it in and we took turns passing it around until we were all flat on our backs on the floor or the couch or wherever in the condo. Now looking around the white condo, the black guys looked like bugs in a cage. They stood out even more than before the drugs. They were like an alien race I didn't want to insult. They must have felt the same because within a few minutes after getting high, they were ready to go back to the Ranch.

Spilling out front, they laced back on their high-tops and piled into the truck. I dropped them out on the edge of their neighborhood and drove back home. Before my girlfriend got home I was asleep. Thank god.

It was the highest I had ever been, and ever wanted to be. I got a first hand lesson in inner city drug abuse. The high was so thrilling I could see how a person would desire to be that way too often, especially if it was the only thrill of the day, week, or life. I never smoked crack again.

Two other incidents occurred while working at the Desert Wharf. Both of these were practically duplications of each other. Besides Julius, there was also a Mexican man of approximately my same age working with us. During the middle of a long shift, he confided in me something his little sister had told him.

He'd caught his sister crying alone in her bedroom. She thought nobody was home and she was all alone. He approached her as a big brother would. Cautiously, he asked her what was wrong. She said that all the good looking boys wanted White girls. They had pretty blonde hair, nice clothes, and got good grades. She said she couldn't compete with the White girls for popularity and that she'd always have to settle for second best. She was ashamed to be Mexican.

The Mexican man was upset with his sister. He explained that she was just as pretty as any White girl. She was just as good as anyone else. This was America and we were all equal.

She complained some more and he hit her.

Julius told me a similar story about a Black girl he knew.

Both stories made me look at racism from the view of people greatly affected by it, by a person who felt powerless to overcome it. I hope both of these girls lost the feeling and found security in who they are. I can only imagine if my sister had said the same things to me and I'm not sure how to respond.

By 1987, I was nearing the end of my school years. But, before I finished college I got a taste of discrimination for myself and I was totally unprepared for it.

I had done about 2-1/2 years at a 2 year school and figured it was time to move on. I had enough credits to transfer to a four year university but wasn't sure how to proceed. I knew it would be expensive and my parents weren't wealthy. They owned the largest bookstore in the area, but it was still only a mom and poop operation.

So I went to see the Dean of Financial Aid and ask for some help. I'd met him a couple times before in my duties as School Trustee and on the newspaper. His name was Luis Corona, a Mexican man who either had a grudge against me personally or all White kids; probably the former.

I made an appointment thru his secretary and a few days later I found myself welcomed into his office. It was small and cramped with barely enough room for two vinyl chairs opposite his large metallic and fake wood desk. Light gray-blue industrial paint covered the walls except for where he had shelves lined with books and folders, thin indoor outdoor carpeting covering the floor.

I took a seat in a vinyl chair and told him I thought it was time for me to move on. I wanted to further my education at a State University, hopefully UCLA, maybe Cal Poly Pomona, or even Humboldt State. If I could just get some help understanding the myriad of grants, loans and scholarships I was sure I could go the next step with my education.

He let me spin my little tale of hopes and dreams, then calmly replied, "Tell your parents to sell a car. There's no help for you here."

I didn't know what to say. I kept waiting for the punch line. But none came. After a short eternity he asked me if there was anything else with a straight face and I knew I was done. So, I left with my tail between my legs.

The semester finished and I had no other plans for school. I'd decided to go even more into the workforce and find a career. I knew I was good at talking to crowds, writing, and had a good general education so I did the obvious thing. I became a car salesman.

Orange Coast Jeep - 1987-1992

Becoming a car salesman meant moving to Orange County. The dealership I was to work at was in Costa Mesa and I'd decided I didn't want to have to take a freeway to work and I wanted to live as close to the beach as I could. Unfortunately, I soon discovered I couldn't afford living too close to the beach just yet.

Leaving Palm Springs, I loaded up 1975 Buick with all my possessions and drove to Costa Mesa. I got a discount motel room with a phone, bought a street map and a newspaper, and began circling the room for rent ads within a 2 mile radius of the dealership. There were lots of rooms available, but based on my lack of confidence in my salesmanship, I decided for the master bedroom of a two bedroom apartment only blocks from the dealership in a shabby neighborhood. My roommates were both Mexican men and one didn't even speak English. Rent was $230 and I was about 4 miles from the beach..

Working at the car dealership was an education. Often, I've said it was like getting a degree in psychology. It was my job to get to know people, learn all the intimacies of their life, discern their needs, figure out where there money is and then rip their life savings away from them, while selling them a car. The problem was, at first, I wasn't good at it. But there were guys who were very good at it.

Men like Johnny Santos, Casey Beckett, Scott Walker and, my personal mentor, Dan Kimberly showed me that a good living can be made at selling cars. All these men were White; as a matter of fact the entire sales force was White. We were Orange County men selling to some of the most affluent people, on average, in the country. It was tough competition and I never minded seeing others succeed at something I was struggling with, because it showed me my goals were possible. Unfortunately, it wasn't until I hit an all-time low that I became determined to be the best salesman I could.

After about a year in the business and never really achieving better than average sales, my numbers began to slide. Within a month or two I finally hit rock bottom and had my worst monthly income since I was a paperboy at 12. I only made $400. It was a moral defeat. I had to make a personal choice to either become the salesman I wanted to be, or get out of car sales.

I chose to improve. I made myself stay on the lot and out of the showroom unless I had a customer. I started reading books on salesmanship, even carrying it with me and reading between customers. And, I started really listening to my bosses and how they talked to customers so I could mimic them. It paid off. Within one month I had made $1400. Not a fortune but a long way from the bottom of the pack and I continued my effort to self-improve my sales ability.

Within a year, I was top salesman. But, at the same time the economy began to slide during the late 1980's and some of the top salesmen began to move to what they thought to be greener pastures. Soon the dealership was short on quality salesmen and the quantity of cars sold by the entire dealership declined. So, the owner changed General Managers.

The new GM had a new philosophy in the type of salesmen he wanted. He preferred to hire a diverse crowd of salespeople. Soon, we had Blacks, Middle Easterners, Mexicans, Asians, a couple of Aussie brothers, and women. We'd gone from a club of Good Old Boys to the United Nations. It was a vastly different environment to sell in. Many of these new salesmen were good too. It didn't matter where they came from, what their heritage or nationality, many of them knew how to sell and since I was top salesman, they made me their mark to beat.

I remember one pair of guys; Mirwas Norzai from Afghanistan and Amir something or other from Iran, who had a tag team approach that was tough to beat.

Mirwas, was extremely friendly and personable. He was slightly pudgy, had a big smile and had this great story of how he played an extra in Rambo III, when Sylvester Stallone joined a small Afghanistani town soccer game using a pigs bladder. He even had the photos to prove it.

Amir, was slender, short, had a small square mustache and smoked constantly. He was the heavy who negotiated price and seldom bent or gave in. Together they excelled at selling.

One month, I had Amir beat by only 1/2 a car for top salesman. We were down to the last few hours of the last day and neither of us would go home so long as the other one was present, or until the store closed. Amir had an advantage because Mirwas was also watching for customers so he could share a deal with Amir. Knowing I had a good chance of being outsold under these conditions I made a gesture of conciliation. I offered to take Mirwas and Amir drinking if we all left together right then. At first they declined, but within a half hour they asked if the offer still stood. We all left together and I was still top salesman.

As the national economy declined during the late 1980's and early 1990's the Japanese and other Oriental economies remained strong. Therefore we saw a substantial influx of Pacific Rim customers; so much so that I had to devise a strategy to sell to these customers.

My first attempt was to fake crying. It happened when this one

Asian man ran me through the ringer; making me drive many cars, refusing for the longest time to pick only one to negotiate on, and then after a long negotiation where he said several times the price he would buy at and my bosses finally succumbed to his low price, then he said he couldn't make a decision because he didn't have his wife. So, when he wasn't looking, I went to the drinking fountain and splashed water in my eyes and pretended to be crying. I shamed him into buying.

The next thing I did right was to earn their respect by merely negotiating a long time and reminding them this was America and we only dealt in American prices and we all had to pay American taxes. This was not my best method to a sale. It was a lot of work and very time nerve wracking and time consuming. But it did work.

Another of my early successes was to make friends with them by show respect using humor. This particular instance involved me sitting with four Asian men who when asked what nationality they were became very stuffy and straight-backed before replying, "we're Vietnamese."

"Really," I exclaimed all happy and excited. "Did you guys see that movie with Robin Williams where he was the disc jockey?" I began to say the name, but they all joined in and very loudly we shouted, "GOOD MORNING VIETNAM!"

The Vietnamese men became very excited and all continued by stating, "Goo Moovy, Goo Moovy."

A sale was made.

Then there was the time that I learned an astounding fact which taught me how to treat both the Asians and the Middle Easterners, who were also tough negotiators.

It was a rainy day. Not just raining, but pouring and Amir had first choice of the next customer. There was a bus stop just off the lot and we watched as a young Oriental man climbed off in a slicker and carrying a backpack. He waded into the used cars.

"He's all yours," I said to Amir.

"I'll pass. You take him," Amir replied. "I can't sell Asians anyways."

I took the customer, who turned out to be an out of country college kid with $5,000 in his backpack who had been told by someone that Orange Coast Jeep was the place to buy a car. A total lay down.

But, I thought on what Amir told me and he was right. I had never seen him sell an Asian, or even take on an Asian customer and I finally figured out the secret to selling both the Asians and the Middle Easterners. I call it the Genghis Khan complex. You see the Chinese and the Arabs shared the same continent long before any White man ventured into Asia. So they share a hatred for each other much more severe than any mistrust of an American. They just all put a chip on their shoulder when they come to put on a show, to try and prevent anyone from taking advantage of them.

So this is what I'd do: When an Asian man would offer me something ridiculous like half price. I would look them square in the eye and say, "what are you Iranian? You're not Iranian are you?"

At which point the Chinaman would get his dander up and say back, "No, me Chinese."

"Well good," I'd answer. "For a second there I thought you were Iranian, because they're the only ones who try and offer me those kind of ridiculous prices. Now let's talk American and send you home in a car."

This strategy worked flawless. The Chinese and the Arabs had been fighting long before a White man ever got between them and allowed me to get a level with them they never expected. They knew what I meant by my words better than I did.

It worked just as good on the Arabs when they'd offer me unreal prices.

"What are you Chinese? Only Chinamen offer those kinds of prices. Let's talk American US Dollars. You did bring American money with you?" My bosses were pleasantly astounded.

To stick with Asians on one more incident; there was this time that we had an Asian salesman named Phan who was pretty good at selling but he was the most obnoxious guy to work with. He always tried to steal your customers, or spoil your deal, and spoke very little English. That is until he left the dealership thinking there was a better place to work.

He came back at the end of the week to pick up his final check and was upset because he thought he was shorted. Suddenly, he spoke great English, perfect English as a matter of fact. And besides, his check wasn't short, he just had some deals that did hold together and he'd been given a fair shake. Unlike the treatment he gave his co-workers.

There were encounters with other types of people also I think are worth noting.

One time I sold a car to these two obvious lesbians; a first for me. I kept my calm through the deal and treated them like anyone else, although not only were they lesbians but one was Black and one was White.

At the end of the deal, during the delivery, I asked the question, "You two don't look like sisters but you have the came last name. How'd that happen?"

"How did that happen?" One said to the other.

The other replied. "We got married."

"You can do that?" I asked seriously.

"Yes," she replied, "in some states."

"Great," I answered and continued showing them how to set the radio stations and where the power seat controls were.

Another time, I had these two inner city guys who were my customers. One was a heavy Mexican dude (Big Tony) and the other a jittery Black guy (JC). They looked like drug dealers or gang members. I really don't know if they were or not though. Big Tony had a truck driving job and was somewhat stable, but JC only had a gas station job. Although they each had $5,000-$8,000 down payment, their credit was a little sketchy, with late payments and collections accounts littering between a little bit of good credit.

I shot straight with them and it probably wasn't the first they'd heard it. They were more than hour from home and there were lots of car dealerships closer to their own neighborhood. I told them exactly why we couldn't finance them even though they had a substantial down. But then I went a step further and told them what I would do if I were in their shoes. I told them to hire a credit repair company. There wasn't anything on their credit report that couldn't be fixed or shaken off by a good repairist. They left thanking me for the advice and I figured that was that.

A little less than a year later they showed up again and they had followed my advice. I was surprised at how well it worked. Big Tony now had what we called Gold Balls and JC was not as good but still good enough to get a car; also, they hadn't blown their down payment. Together they both left with brand new Jeep Cherokees and over the next week they came back and fixed them up. Whereas most people raise their Jeeps with suspension lifts, JC and Big Tony lowered theirs all the way to the ground. They replaced their large spongy steering wheels with miniature chain link steering wheels and tinted all the windows, which kind of surprised me. Because at one point in the selection process JC kept telling me I need a car with a light interior.

I kept showing him the tan interior thinking it to be the lightest.

"No," he said. "Want light."

"But, it is light," I'd say.

"You don't get it man," he'd say making his point. "See brother, I'm black and if I don't have a light interior nobody is going to see me in the car. And in a car likes this, I wants to be seen."

I finally understood and showed him a jeep with the light gray interior. He loved it. They turned out to be great guys and great customers. I even remember their low rider jeeps rubbing the driveway on the way out in their way home.

Then there was George, a Mexican man of enormous size. George was at least 6'3" tall and easily weighed 250 pounds. He wasn't fat, just large.

One day, we were all comparing handshakes and greetings. Seeing who had the best ability to take control of the customers' right from the start. Any of the good salesmen had a pretty good handshake but when George shook your hand he first shook with his right hand and then covered yours and his both with his left. It felt like someone had just placed your hand in a freshly baked loaf of bread. It was all warm and spongy and the last thing you wanted to do was take it out of the oven. George had control. He was also a spectacular salesman who spoke fluent Spanish. He used his bilingual ability to keep himself at the top of the sales board constantly. But he only took the job until he could resolve some legal troubles and once those were handled he moved on.

My sales had improved so much I became eligible for management but kept being overlooked for more mature men. My opportunity finally came when the General Manager told me he wanted to get rid of the oldest man at the dealership, Vit. Vit was a customer care employee who made follow-up calls to purchasers and service customers, asking them how they were treated, did they get all their questions answered, and how happy they were. He was easily 70 years old and none of the other managers wanted to be the one to tell the old guy that he didn't have a job anymore.

I don't know why the GM wanted to get rid of Vit, but he told me, "If you can fire Vit, I'll make you a manager."

I immediately went out and told Vit he had to go. Vit put up a little bit of a fight, saying he thought he should talk to the GM, but I tld him, "I wouldn't be out here if I didn't have his approval already." Vit grabbed his briefcase and took off down the sidewalk to catch his bus, never to be seen again. I was promoted to manager within a day, at the age of 24., but it wouldn't last. I wasn't ready. It took me several times of going up and down the ladder before I started to get the hang of leading a team of salesmen. Eventually I got the hang of it, but not yet.

The best friend I ever made at the dealership was a Mexican man of my same age. His name is Robert Muratella. Robert was so much fun to be with that I seldom wanted to separate from him. We worked side by side, both as salesmen at first. Then I got promoted and he worked for me. But he had talent and was soon promoted himself. He was the kind of guy who married his high school sweetheart and never moved too far his parents and although he knew when to pass the blame, you couldn't help but love him. Because he'd do it in such an obvious way that anyone involved knew what he doing, but he so much darn fun that you'd let him.

During the slow times, when good salesmen were hard to find and maintaining strong sales was even harder, Robert's wife wanted him to move onto a better job. Several times he quit car sales to begin a new career, and each time my upper managers sent me after him to entice him back. He would come back too. But eventually, I wore out my welcome in my house because unknowingly I was overly straining his marriage and I've always felt bad about that. If I could apologize to anyone and rekindle a friendship with anyone from my past, it would be Robert and his wife Nancy.

Another great friend I made, was the only salesman to ever consistently exceed me once I'd hit the top of my game; he's an Indian man, (from India not North America) who grew up in London and spoke with a British accent. The effect was quite baffling on customers and even confused me at first before I became used to it. His name is Bruce Gajjar and he still works for Orange Coast at the time of this writing.

Bruce is a brilliant salesman who can spot a persons needs and desires and works tirelessly to fill them. Never afraid of a long shift or helping out, he was instant manager material but he tactfully refused it until he knew there was no better competition for the post. His strategy was that once he made manager he didn't want the prospect of ever losing it. When I need advice on an auto purchase, I still call Bruce.

Together, Bruce, Robert and I were the mangers at the dealership during one of the happiest times of my life. Money was good, friends were abundant, and my job was challenging yet fun. We also jointly wrote my first book. It was the sales training manual for the dealership. It was only about thirty pages long but it went over every aspect of the sale from Meet and Greet to the Delivery and Follow-up. It explained the entire approach the Orange Coast way. I was told it was required reading for all new recruits for years to come.

Eventually though I decided to move on. I thought I was ready to run the entire dealership and the owner told me I had a long way to go before the next promotion was due. There were plenty of older more experienced men available to fill the upper management positions and so, I decided it was time to go. I let my attitude deflate, my sales slip and I moved back to the desert to find a new career.

But before I went back to the desert I decided to take a trip to the East Coast. I had made friends years earlier when I worked for the Chart House with Kevin Hooper and we had kept in touch occasionally. He'd always told me that I was welcome to visit him and this felt like a good destination to get away to. I booked a flight, landed at Baltimore-Washington International Airport and made my way to his place, a small row house near a Colonial battle site called Fort McHenry.

Kevin wanted to show me the town, only he'd changed since I'd known him last. Now he was gay. He took me to a club in Washington DC called TRACKS. It was huge, boasting three dance rooms and a volleyball court. It was the first time I ever saw anyone who had their nipples pierced.

The next night we went to a bar in Baltimore called The Hippo Room. We met a couple of girls there but they turned out to be Lesbians. We asked them if they had any advice one different places to go. They asked, "Straight or Gay?"

"Could go either way," I answered, thinking Kevin is gay and I'm straight. They mentioned a place that we went to but didn't stay long. Kevin wanted to smoke some pot and told me who knew a place nearby. We ended up on a deserted lot overlooking the inner-harbor. He rolled a joint lit it and passed it to me.

I took a hit and Kevin pushed me back in my seat. I was confused but trusted my friend until he laid his head in my lap. I protested but Kevin had my zipper down quick and my member in his mouth an instant later. I smoked the rest of the joint while my childhood friend blew me. When he finished he threw his arms around my neck and I told him, "I can't return that favor." He didn't care and kissed my cheek. Then he asked if there was any pot left.

Later, I went out cruising on my own and found a prostitute. She was Black. We went to another deserted lot and performed missionary style in the backseat. I needed to confirm to myself I was still straight.

The Book Business 1992-2000

Arriving back in Palm Springs, I didn't have much of a plan. For two years I worked for my Dad at the two local swap meets. At one, we sold sunglasses. It was on the weekend and we had to get up at 4:30 in the morning and work till 3 in the afternoon. At the other, we started at 5 in the evening and worked until 11 PM selling used books. The pay was pretty good for working three days a week at about $350. But it was no fortune and no career.

Palm Springs had changed during my absence; there was now a substantial Gay population. There's a Gay hotel district and a gay business district. One business went so far as to call itself GAYMART.

It specializes in all things Gay; books, clothes, sexual aids, postcards, all sorts of stuff. Bars specializing in gay clientele are packed. One of the biggest events in the city is a weekend festival called the White Party, which is a draw for homosexuals to converge from all over the country. There's even an annual Gay Pride parade.

Entire neighborhoods were decidedly Gay. Areas that used to be run down have been bought out, fixed up and filled with Gay couples. Even around the home I live in now, two of my three neighbors are Gay. I have mixed feelings on this. Even though I had that one encounter with Kevin, I have no desire to repeat it. I tolerate the Gays, I even like quite a few of them, and have some really great friends. But, I can't help but think it still isn't right.

But, live and let live. I do try and consider the possibility that I may not always be right. After all, I don't run the world and what happened to me soon after moving back to Palm Springs proved this to be true.

The most serious minority encounter of the time was what happened to our Thursday night book booth in Palm Springs. The city council was going to change the rules governing the event to outlaw books from being a saleable product. We were no longer going to be allowed to sell books at the street fair called Villagefest.

My dad and I prepared a strategy to fight City Hall. We argued at Parks & recreation and Villagefest commission meetings, but to no avail. Commissioners had it in their heads that used book were bringing a lower class of citizen to the event and that books weren't collectible enough; or at least that's what they were saying. I was a ludicrous argument, but they weren't budging.

So, Dad and I moved our public speaking to City Council sessions on Wednesday evenings. We made a pilgrimage of it, speaking every week. Sometimes we'd write one long speech and read it in succession handing the script off from one to the other when our three minutes would expire.

But, it wasn't until we hit on the theme of minority discrimination that we began to score points. The Mayor was a Jewish man and when we compared the book banning to another great act of book banning that had occurred fifty years earlier in the world. He suggested the rules be changed to allow for books that are at least twenty years old.

We then changed our speeches to suggest what types of people had only come into public acceptance in the last twenty years. Blacks, Hispanics, and women had only recently started gaining recognition in literature and how dare the Council try and hide their histories from a desiring public.

At this point, my dad and I knew we had them on the run. Besides we were becoming a popular show in the community. The City Council meetings are televised and we now had name recognition. People were coming up to us on Thursday nights and introducing themselves, telling us they enjoyed our speeches and wishing they had the balls to stand up to City Hall like we were.

The Mayor was feeling the pressure too and decided to fight back. He was nearing the end time of the old rules and the day was near for the implementation of the new rules. Since he wasn't getting his way, he determined the Council should go with the original draft of just outlawing book sales all together at the weekly event.

I was furious and I drafted the most scathing speech I had to date. My dad and I talked it over and we were ready to go to court. On the night of the meeting when a Council decision was to be made I got sick, probably due to the stress of the situation. My dad gave the speech I wrote and basically it said, "Go ahead and change the rules if you think you're right. Because we think the law will favor us. On Thursday night we're setting up in our normal spot regardless of what the rules say. So send out you're jack booted thugs and try to close us down and you'll go down as the Mayor and City who tried to ban books." We were done talking.

The Council postponed the issue instead of approving it and the City Manager told me a day later that the rules would get changed in our favor at the next meeting.

At the next meeting the item was not on the agenda, so I confronted the Mayor nose to nose during one of the intermission breaks and cussed at him, asking what kind of "Bullshit" he was trying to prove. We're serious, I told him. If it wasn't on the agenda in a week and if he didn't follow through on the promise of acceptance, we were prepared to start our own lawsuit.

It was a small item, mixed in with half a dozen other things and treated like it was an item of unimportance, but we got approved.

Then one day something really happened to change my life and give me direction.

I was at Ralph's supermarket buying some groceries and there was a special display of comic books. It was the Death of Superman issue where Superman fights a monster called Doomsday and dies in the process. In the end, Superman lies in Lois Lanes arms battered, bloody and deceased while she sobs and in the background his tattered cape hangs from a broken pole like a defeated flag. It was spectacular and that storyline revived the comic industry for a couple years. I bought all 6 copies in the rack and shortly thereafter became a comic book dealer.

Within a year, I grew to over 30,000 comics and was still growing. My dad, watched me buy collections, make a profit and end up with more comics every week. At the end of that year, he offered to go in partners on a used book store. He would supply a bounty of used books and I would supply the comics and the day to day running of the store. A landlord made us a deal on rent if we'd go with a Hollywood name and Celebrity Bookstore was born.

At the store one day I had a group of black kids come in and one of them stole an armful of comics, literally running out of the store at a sprint and making no pretense of acting innocent. I ran to the door to try and catch him but didn't want to abandon the store with his friends still inside. So instead, I turned on them and made them stay in the store until I called the cops. I was outnumbered four to one and any two of them could probably take me; especially this one who had the athletic build of a running back. Although they wouldn't confess to being accomplices to the one who stole my comics.

They did offer to work off the price of the books their friend stole. Two of them even came back several times and asked for more work and turned out to be pretty good guys and them were the two who seemed to have the least opportunities available.

The bookstore went fine for a while, and then the landlord went greedy and wanted rent increases I felt were unjustified. Also, I was informed by the property manager that City officials had asked the landlord not to be agreeable to us as revenge for losing the Villagefest book issue. So, I closed down the store. It made me cry.

But, it did allow me to concentrate on the internet and within 6 months I had the operation performing nicely in a new direction. A month later I met the woman who was to become my wife, Tracey Wrubleski, a realtor from Palm Desert and really great lady. With her help, I bought a house and two years later we were married and opening another store, only this time it was called Celebrity Books.com.

Tracey's family is a mixed bag of nuts. Not only are they a fun bunch to be around but, they also have several different races who have married in. There's a Japanese/Hawaiian brother-in-law and a Black brother-in-law. There's also a Latino sister-in-law and a cousin who married an East Indian, and they're all really fantastic people. I've told most of them about my writing this story and it didn't bother any of them. As a matter of fact, when I told them of the Dean of Financial Aid rejecting my request for help completing college, they appeared to understand that discrimination can go both ways.

Now, Tracey and I are thinking of adopting kids. We'd like to have a couple of them, siblings would be nice. Tracey has her own son, Brahm, now 17. I've never had any. We thought of having our own but I've had sex with lots of women and never had anything come of it and Tracey had her tubes tied about 10 years ago. We could have them untied and seek medical help but there's always the chance that it would take several attempts and each try costs about 10 grand. So, instead we decided to adopt.

I only had one criterion for adoption; that the kids look like us. If you didn't know Tracey and I are both White with blonde hair. Friends, family and the social worker jump to the conclusion that the kids have to have blue eyes too, although that's not true. They don't even have to be blonde. So long as they're fair haired and skinned. Brown, blonde, sandy, even a little red-headed child is just fine by me. Tracey won't take a red head though. She would take a darker skinned child than me, but I'm adamant in my parameters.

Unfortunately, the area we're in doesn't have many fair headed kids. Most of the kids that become available through the County Adoption program are Mexican or Black, which doesn't work for me.

I don't consider this a racial thing though: It's not discrimination in my mind. I think this is a very personal decision on our parts. This is a decision we only want to say yes to once. We do't want to have any returns or rejections. It's the most important decision I can imagine any person making and I want to make sure it's the right one when we make it.

We should look like a family unit in my mind. We won't hide the fact that the kids were adopted. When the time comes to share the information we will. But, I also don't want any unnecessary questions raised by any other kids or schoolmates. I only hope I can provide for them the same or better life than my parents gave me.

www.ingramcontent.com/pod-product-compliance
Lightning Source LLC
Chambersburg PA
CBHW060635290526
45793CB00001B/255